A is for Archery

Archery is one of the oldest hunting skills in the world — people have used bows and arrows for thousands of years!

B
is for Bear

Bears sleep through the winter in dens — it's called hibernation.

is for Camo

Camo helps hunters blend into the woods so animals can't see them.

D

is for Deer

A white-tailed deer raises its tail like a flag when it runs away!

E is for Elk

Bull elk make a loud sound called a bugle — it echoes through the mountains!

G is for Ground blind

Ground Blinds look like small tents and blend into the woods!

H
is for Hunter

Good hunters are patient, quiet, and respectful of nature.

I is for Instinct

Animals use instinct to survive — like knowing when to run or hide!

is for Jerky

Jerky is a tasty trail snack made from dried meat.

K is for Kodiak

Kodiak bears are one of the biggest bears in the world!

is for Labrador

Labradors are friendly dogs that love to fetch and swim!

M

is for Moose

Even though they're big, moose can swim really well!

is for Nock

The nock is the small notch at the end of an arrow that clips onto the bowstring.

is for Oak Tree

Oak trees grow strong and tall, and their acorns feed deer, turkeys, and squirrels.

P

is for Pack

Some hunters use a pack to carry out meat after a harvest.

is for Quiver

Archery hunters use a quiver to keep their arrows organized and ready to shoot.

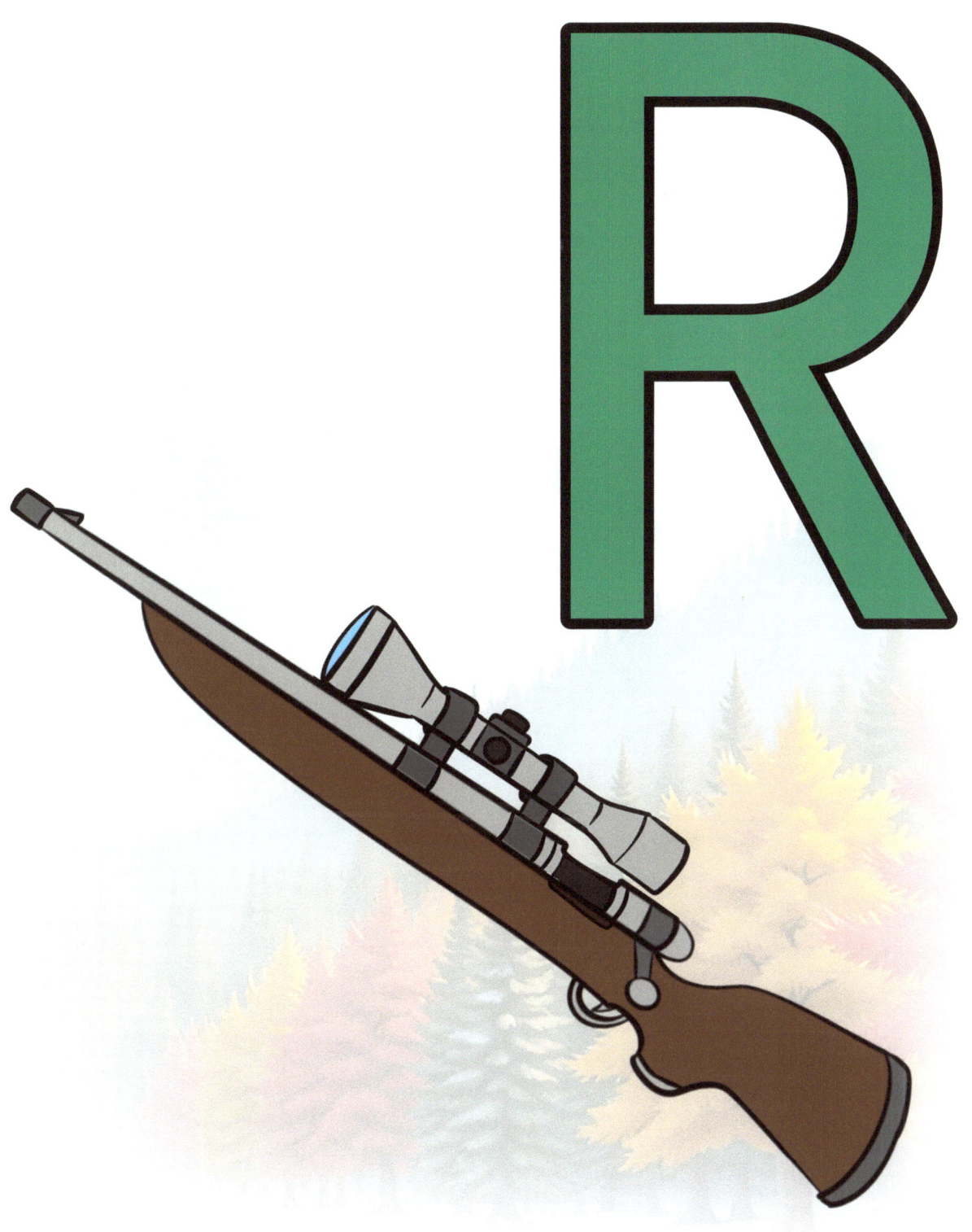

is for Rifle

Rifles help hunters make clean, careful shots.

S is for Squirrel

Squirrels use their fluffy tails for balance and to keep warm!

T is for Treestand

Treestands help hunters stay hidden high in the trees!

is for Upland

Upland birds like pheasants and grouse live in tall grass and fields.

is for Vest

Blaze orange vests help hunters stay safe and visible to others.

W
is for Wildlife

Wildlife means all the animals that live in nature — from bears to birds!

Fo<u>x</u> ends with X

A fox can sneak through the woods without making a sound!

Y
is for Yearling

A yearling is a young deer that's about one year old.

is for Zipper

Zippers help keep tents closed and the bugs out!

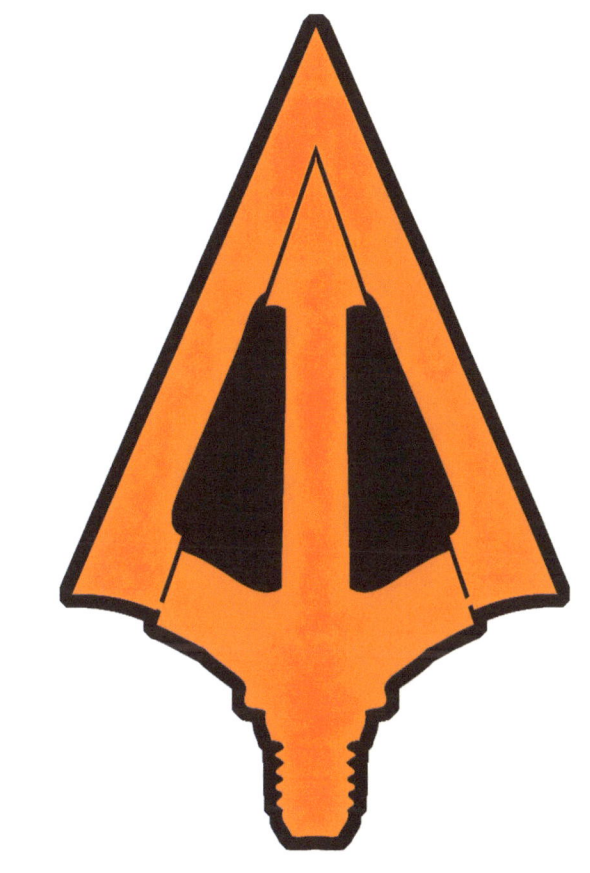

www.ingramcontent.com/pod-product-compliance
Lightning Source LLC
Chambersburg PA
CBHW061157030426
42337CB00002B/37